2nd Edition

Includes Free
Downloadable Recordings!

Helen Marlais

Succeeding at the Piano®
A Method for Everyone

Let's Play!

T0008845

WHAT YOU NEED

A piano or an 88-key keyboard

The desire to learn

Time to practice

Your imagination!

COMPOSERS

Timothy Brown

Kevin Costley

Mary Leaf

Helen Marlais

Edwin McLean

Kevin Olson

Production: Frank J. Hackinson
Production Coordinators: Peggy Gallagher and Philip Groeber
Editors: Edwin McLean, Peggy Gallagher, Joyce Loke and
    Nancy Bona-Baker
Art Direction: Andi Whitmer and Sandy Brandvold – in collaboration
    with Helen Marlais
Cover Illustration: © 2010 Susan Hellard/Arena
Interior Illustrations: © 2010 Susan Hellard/Arena and
    © 2015, 2016 Teresa Robertson/Arena
Cover and Interior Illustration Concepts: Helen Marlais
Engraving: Tempo Music Press, Inc.
Printer: Tempo Music Press, Inc.

ISBN-13: 978-1-61928-158-5

THE
F·J·H
MUSIC
COMPANY
INC.
Frank J. Hackinson

TABLE OF CONTENTS

COMPOSERS AND ARRANGERS

Timothy Brown:	Student solos: p. 8, 12, 14, 17, 18 Lyrics: p. 8, 17, 18 Duet parts: p. 12, 14, 17, 18
Kevin Costley:	Student solos: p. 6, 16, 23 Lyrics: p. 3, 6, 16, 23 Duet parts: p. 6
Mary Leaf:	Student solos: p. 10, 24 Lyrics: p. 24 Duet parts: p. 10, 24
Helen Marlais:	Student solos: p. 3, 4, 5, 7, 19, 20, 22 Lyrics: p. 3, 7, 22 Duet part: p. 3
Edwin McLean:	Student solos: p. 10, 22 Lyrics: p. 10, 22 Duet parts: p. 4, 5, 7, 10, 20
Kevin Olson:	Duet part: p. 22

The composers of the classical pieces are listed under the titles:
p. 5 (*Fun in Our Fort* - Joseph Küffner, 1776-1856)
p. 12 (*Spanish Dance* - El Fandango - E C. de Marescot)
p. 14 (*Theme from the "London" Symphony* - Franz Joseph Haydn, 1732-1809)
p. 20 (*Waterfalls* - Ferdinand Beyer, 1803-1863)

FJH2270

UNIT 1

Practice steps:

- Circle all the skips. Skips are also called 3rds.
- Draw a triangle (△) around the only Guide Note Bass F.

 TRACK 2, 3, 4

Listen to My Story Now

C Position

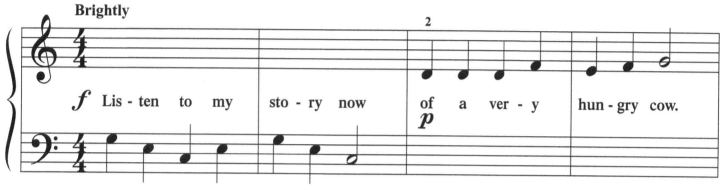

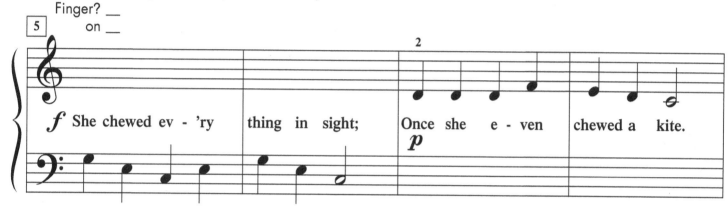

DUET PART: (student plays 1 octave higher)

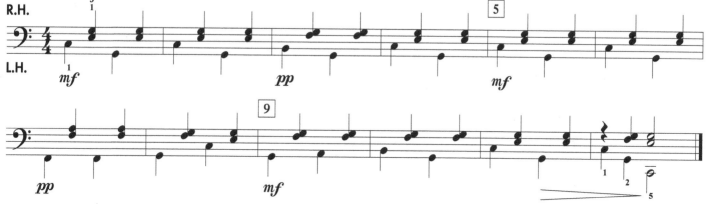

UNIT 2

Practice steps:

- Tap and count aloud.
- Circle the six dynamic marks.
  Plan how they will sound.

The Pony Ride

Flemish Folk Song

TRACK 5, 6, 7

Riding along

f We all ride on our po - nies, our *mp*

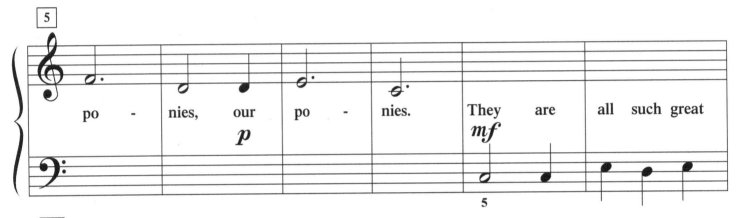

po - nies, our po - nies. They are all such great
p *mf*

beau - ties; we love to ride. *mp*
f

- Did you hear the dynamic changes?

DUET PART: (student plays 1 octave higher)

R.H.

L.H. *mf* *p* *pp*

mp *mf* *p*

FJH2270

Practice steps:

- Circle the skips.
- Tap and count aloud.

Fun in Our Fort
Op. 168, No. 29
Joseph Küffner (1776-1856)

TRACK 8, 9, 10

With spirit

Roll off the key, wrist first.

getting louder

Roll off the key, wrist first.

DUET PART: (student plays 1 octave higher)

Practice steps:

- Your hand moves each time this pattern occurs: ♩ ♩ ♩ 𝄾
- Play the piece silently.

Jumpin' Jan

With confidence

mf Jump-in' Jan | al - ways jumped | when she went out - side to play.

In her house, | on her bed, | on her tram-po - | line each day.

Then one day *p* | Jan jumped high, *mp* | right up - on a | cloud. *getting louder*

mf Wow, how cool and | awe - some! | Jump-in' Jan *f* | was so proud!

DUET PART: (student plays 1 octave higher)

R.H.

L.H. *mp* with pedal

cresc. *mp*

Practice steps:

- Tap and count aloud.
- Plan the slurs.

On My Bike

TRACK 14, 15, 16

Zipping along

mf Tak - ing a ride on my bike,

Be - ing out - side's what I like.

p Down the hills, up the hills, *getting louder* whis - tling a tune,

mf When I bike ride in the af - ter - noon.

- Did you hear the slurs?
- Can you memorize this piece?

DUET PART: (student plays 1 octave higher)

R.H.

L.H. *mp*

pp   *mp*

- This piece tells a story of a giant lumberjack. Imagine the story while you play it.

- Two musical patterns that are the same are marked with a ✓. Can you find the others?

TRACK 17, 18, 19

The Story of Paul Bunyan

With energy!

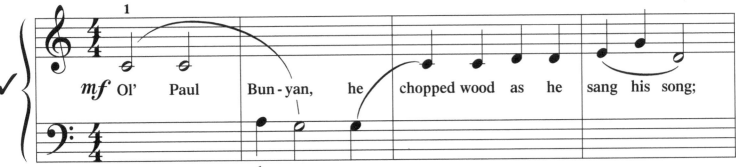

mf Ol' Paul Bun-yan, he chopped wood as he sang his song;

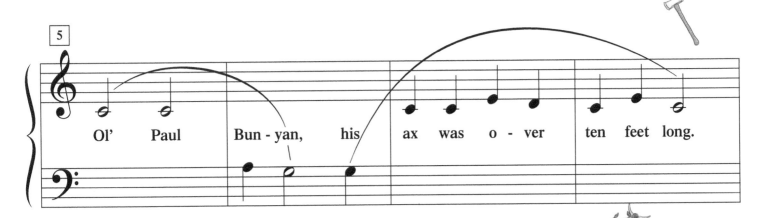

Ol' Paul Bun-yan, his ax was o-ver ten feet long.

Look ahead and move down!

He was big and he was strong, his ox Babe would come a-long.

f

Babe would al-ways pull the wood; she just al-ways un-der-stood.

getting louder

8va both hands 1 octave lower - - - - - - - - - -

8

FJH2270

Roll off the keys, wrists first, and place them in your lap.

move L.H.

• Imagine the story while you play. Doing this will bring the music to life!

Practice steps:

- Tap hands together and count.
- Use a "**Drip-Drop-Roll**" motion that you know for the slurs.

Down at the Lakeside

Moving along

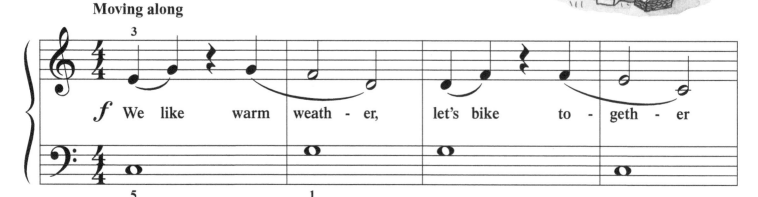

We like warm weath - er, let's bike to - geth - er

Down to the lake - side; it's not far a - way.

DUET PART: (student plays 1 octave higher)

FJH2270

Remember your  and

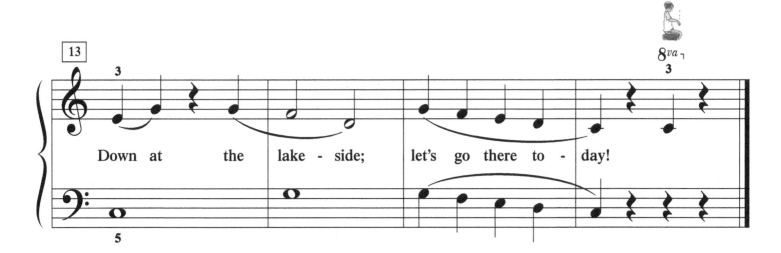

- Did you hear the quarter rests?
- Did you play with a flexible wrist for the two-note slurs?

Practice steps:

- Tap and count the rhythm aloud.
- Circle the only A in the right hand.

TRACK 23, 24, 25

Spanish Dance
Op. 42
Charles de Marescot

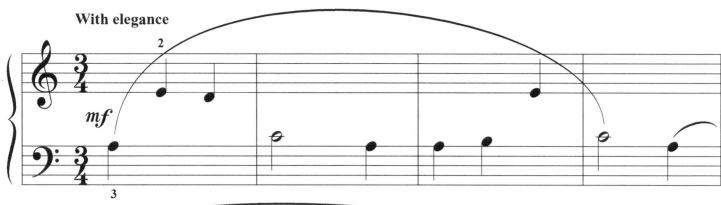

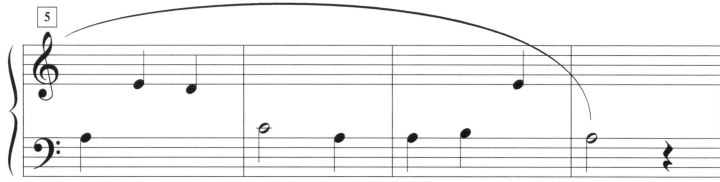

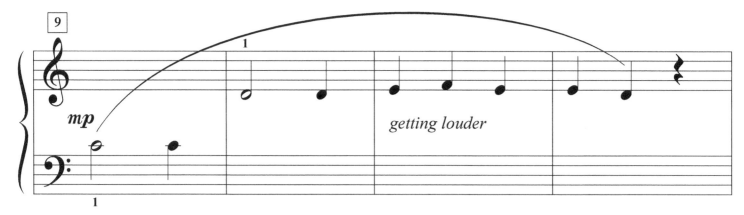

DUET PART: (student plays 1 octave higher)

FJH2270

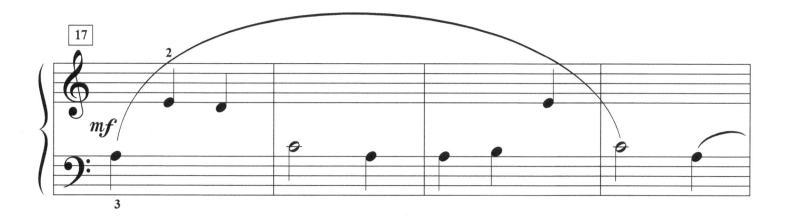

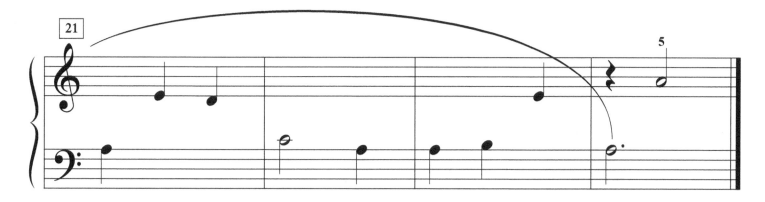

- Were the notes under the slurs *legato*?
- Did the piece flow like a dance?

Practice steps:

- Tell your teacher which musical patterns are the same in this piece.

- Use a woodpecker touch release for the *staccato* notes.

 TRACK 26, 27, 28

Theme from the "London" Symphony

Symphony No. 104, Movement Four
by Franz Joseph Haydn (1732-1809)

A theme is an important melody. Can you hum this theme?

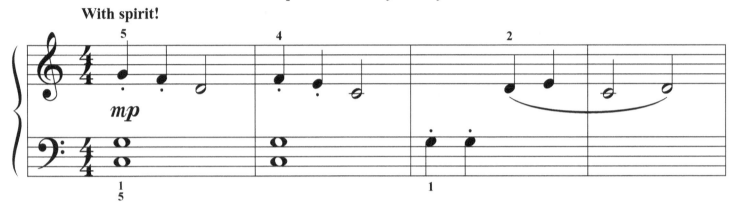

DUET PART: (student plays 1 octave higher)

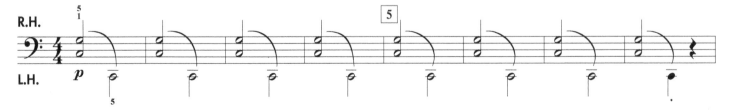

FJH2270

Papa Haydn traveled to London, England to premiere (first perform) twelve pieces he wrote for orchestra, called the "London" Symphonies. The people of London loved Haydn and his music! Haydn is considered to be the "father of the symphony."

- How did the staccato notes feel? How did they sound?
- How did the notes within the slurs feel and sound?

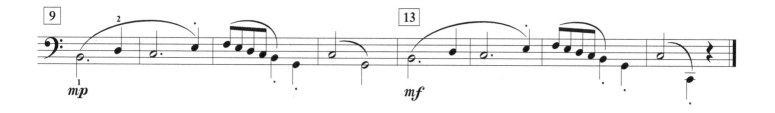

Practice steps:

- Tap the rhythm and count aloud.
- Circle and plan the 4ths.

We're on a Road Trip

With spunk

mf We're on a road trip, we're fi - n'lly on our way;

Head - ed for the o - cean, on the beach to play.

Oh what fun *p* *mp* we will have *mf* rid - ing those big waves!

This week on the *mp* *mf* beach will be *f* one big hol - i - day! *R.H.*

FJH2270

Practice step:

- Circle and block (play together) the 4ths in the music.

 TRACK 32, 33, 34

My Favorite Colors

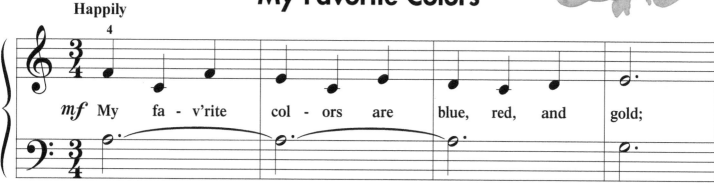

Happily

mf My fa - v'rite col - ors are blue, red, and gold;

My fa - v'rite col - ors are bright and so bold.

getting louder

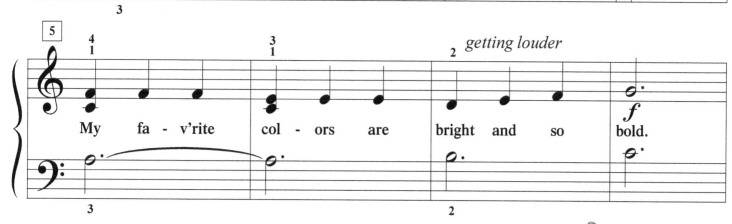

My fa - v'rite col - ors just nev - er get old.

getting softer

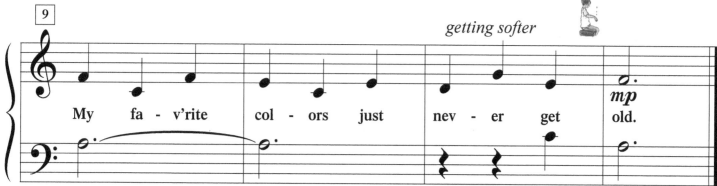

- Can you memorize this piece?

DUET PART: (student plays 1 octave higher)

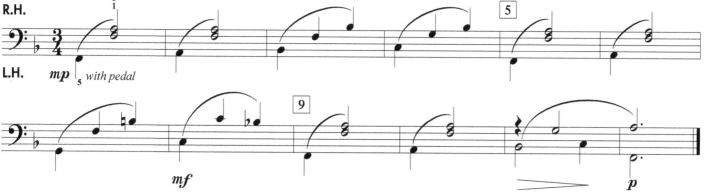

R.H.

L.H. mp with pedal

mf

Practice step:

- Play each line slowly at least three times.

Giants Jumping!

With a heavy beat

f Gi - ants jump - ing off the ground, what a crash - ing, smash - ing sound!

They are jump - ing all a - round, gi - ants jump - ing off the ground.

Oh no, *mp* *getting louder* they are run - ning, sounds like thun - der crash - ing down. *mf*

Push off, wrists first

Gi - ants jump - ing *mp getting louder* off the ground, what a crash - ing *f* smash - ing sound!

DUET PART: (student plays 1 octave higher)

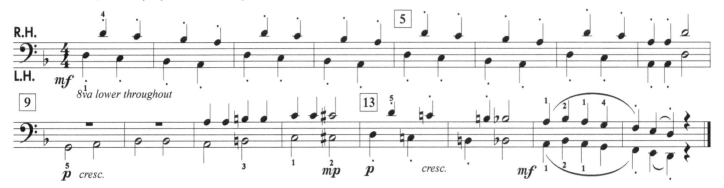

R.H.

L.H. *mf*

8va lower throughout

p *cresc.* *mp* *p* *cresc.* *mf*

FJH2270

Practice steps:

- Play the 1st line, R.H. alone, correctly 5 times.
- Think about using a free arm with strong fingers.
- Then, hands together, practice by "units" – 1 measure plus 1 downbeat.
- Add 4 phrases to the music (one over each line).

Let's Plant a Garden

Traditional Flemish

TRACK 38, 39, 40

Practice steps:

- Both hands play in _____ clef.
- The melody is in the _____ hand.
- Bring out the melody over the L.H. harmony.
  This is called "balancing the melody."

TRACK 41, 42, 43

Waterfalls
Ferdinand Beyer (1803-1863)

DUET PART: (student plays 1 octave higher)

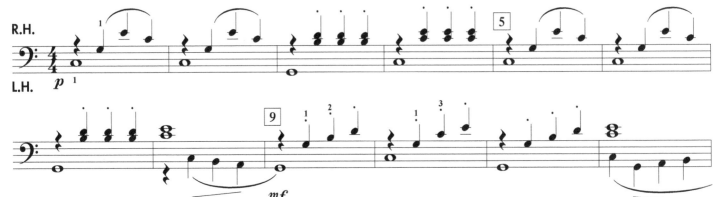

FJH2270

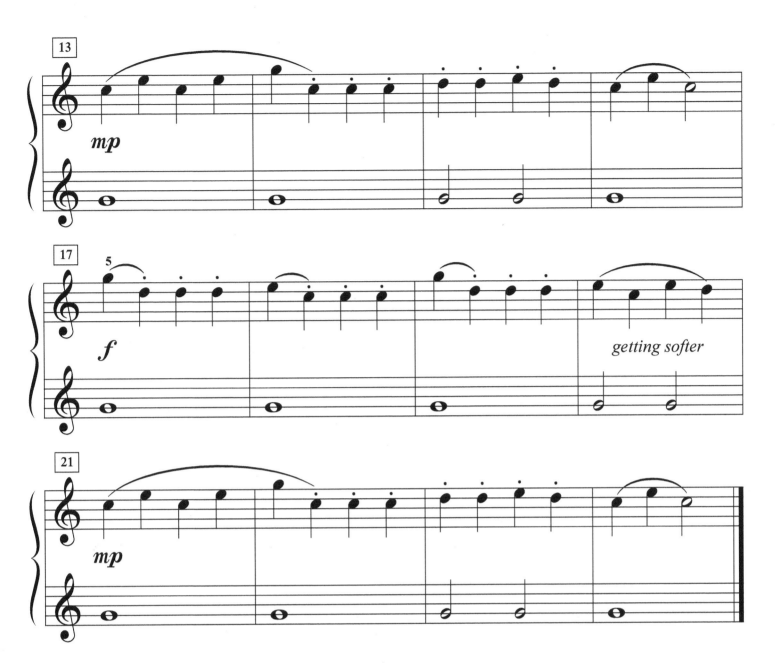

- Did the piece flow quickly?
- Can you memorize this piece?

- Experiment with  and touch releases for the *staccato* notes. Which release sounds better? Which one feels better?

Practice steps:

- Notice that your left hand plays in the Treble staff.
- Sit between Treble C and Treble G.

What Is It?

With motion

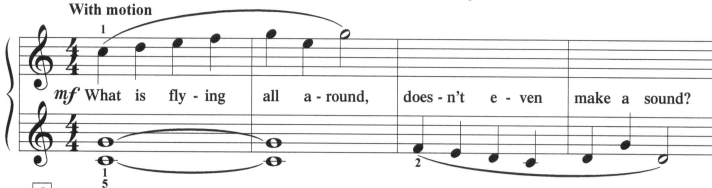

What is fly - ing all a - round, does - n't e - ven make a sound?

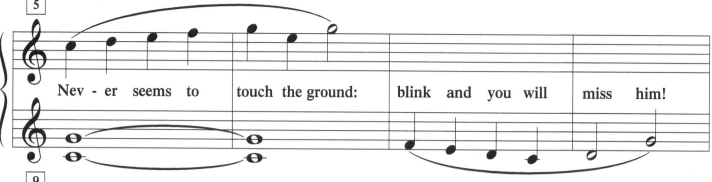

Nev - er seems to touch the ground: blink and you will miss him!

Wings that beat real - ly fast, ti - ny thing whiz-zing past.

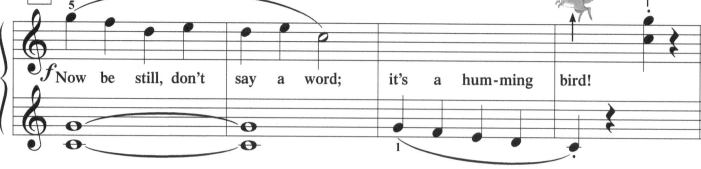

Now be still, don't say a word; it's a hum-ming bird!

DUET PART: (student plays as written)

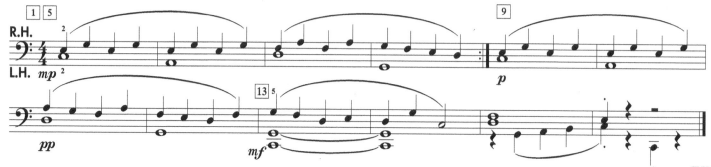

R.H.

L.H.

FJH2270

UNIT 8

Practice steps:

- Circle the half rests.
  How many are there? _____

Let's Go to the Pool

Walking along

mp When it's hot the pool is not, so let's go to the pool!

5

mf You don't have to bring a raft, but they are real ly cool.

9

I have lo - tion just for you, floats and balls and gog - gles too.

13

mp While you're talk - ing, I'll start walk - ing to the swim - ming pool!

TRACK 50, 51, 52

Dancing Shoes

Lively

move both hands down

mf Hear the fid - dles play - ing, while ev' - ry - bod - y's sway - ing, we've

got our danc - ing shoes on, we're at the barn dance!

DUET PART: (student plays 1 octave higher)

R.H.

L.H.

FJH2270

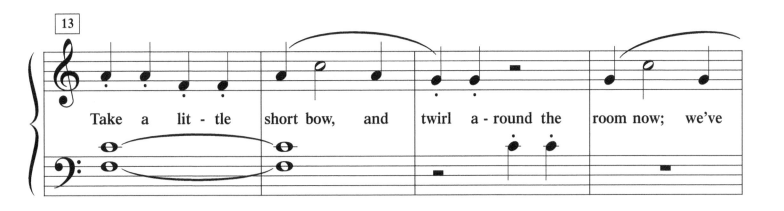

Take a lit-tle short bow, and twirl a-round the room now; we've

got our danc-ing shoes on, we're at the barn dance!

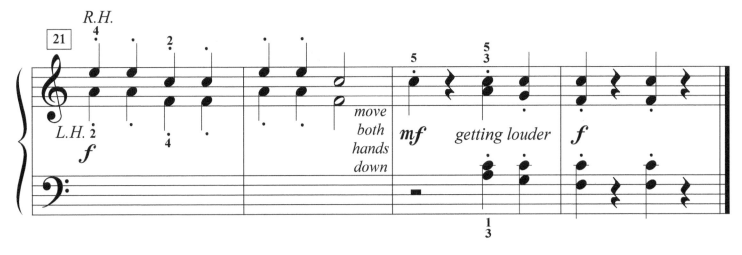

move both hands down *mf* *getting louder* *f*

Pieces I have performed:

Write the pieces you have performed from this book.

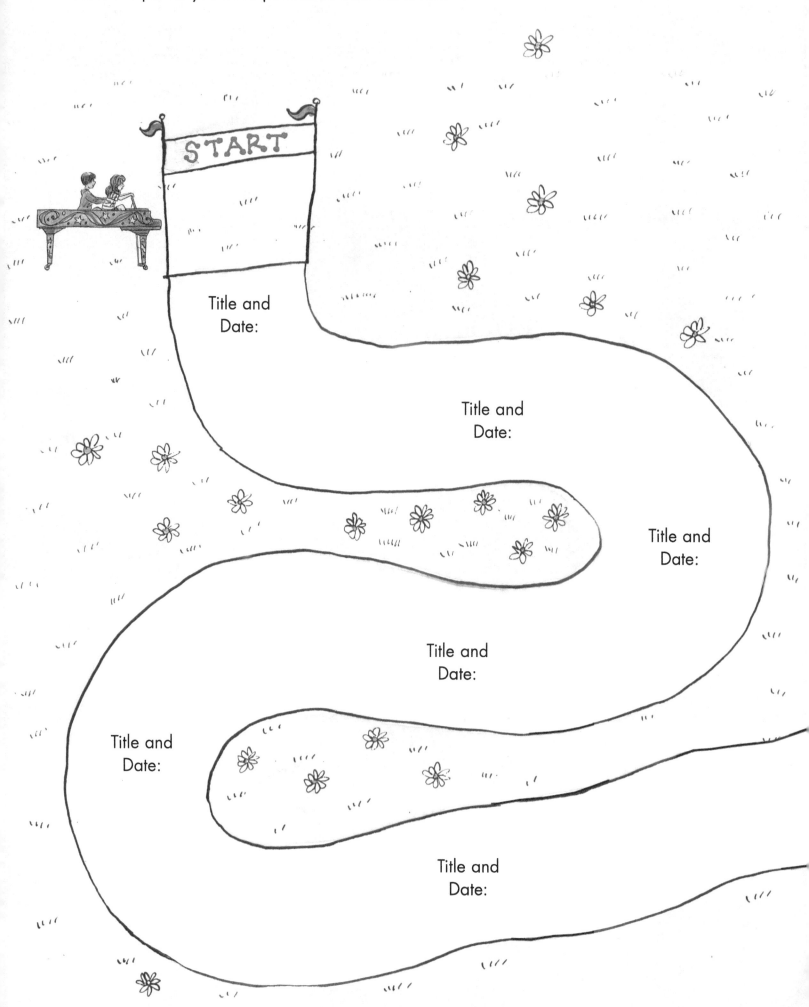

START

Title and
Date:

Title and
Date:

Title and
Date:

Title and
Date:

Title and
Date:

Title and
Date:

FJH2

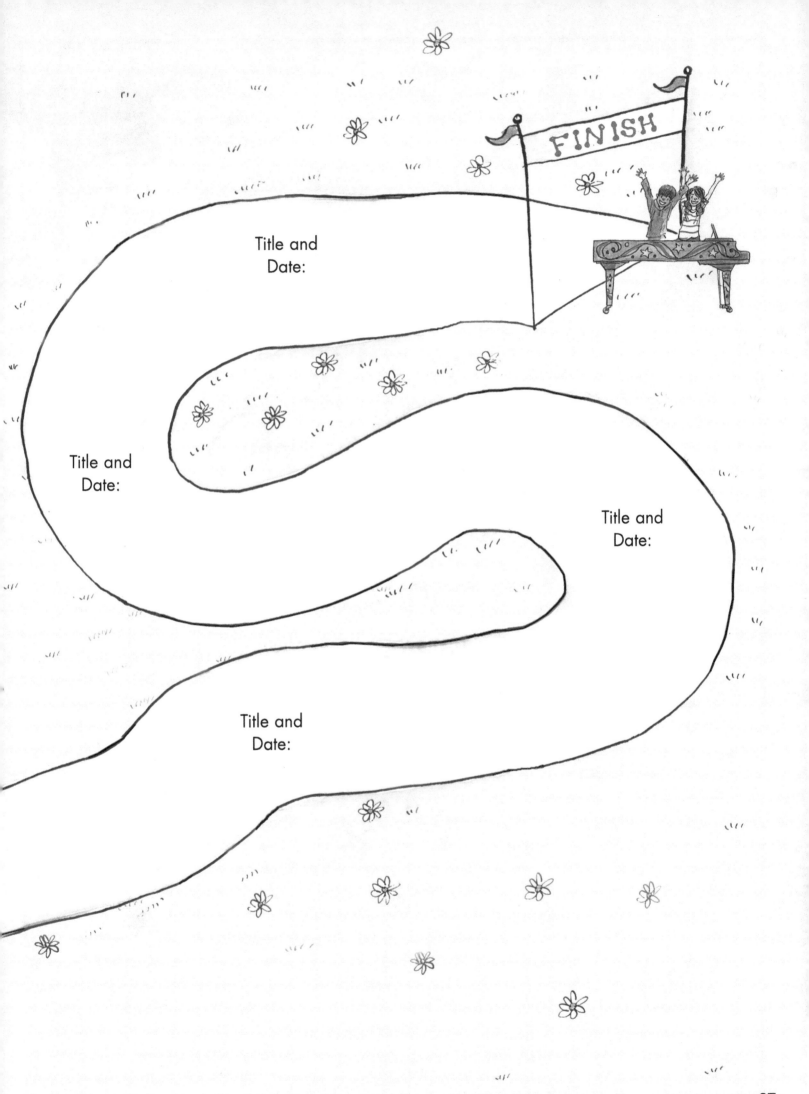

Title and
Date:

Title and
Date:

Title and
Date:

Title and
Date:

FINISH

Certificate of Achievement

_____

Student

has completed

Succeeding at the Piano®
by Helen Marlais

Recital Book
GRADE 1A

You are now ready for
GRADE 1B

_____   _____

Date   Teacher's Signature

THE
F·J·H
MUSIC
COMPANY
INC.

Frank J. Hackinson